The Rant

Shahrzad Hamzeh

Contents

Preface

I've been torn about sharing this, knowing that some people will laugh or say, "I told you so." Others might blame themselves for not seeing my pain or question why I didn't reach out for help. I understand that some will be upset and may react harshly, but it's hard to ask for help when you feel there's none available.

For those who might ask why I spoke of love while describing the pain I endured, the point of this story is that I didn't understand what true love was. I didn't realize that love should also be something I receive, not just give.

This isn't just about coming from a different country and culture. Many people here and now are experiencing similar struggles. I'm sharing this to let them know they are not alone and that love should never be painful.

Please be aware that this discussion revolves around an abusive relationship. If you think it might be triggering for you, please stop reading now.

If you are going through something similar and you feel like you're stuck and that my situation is greatly different from what you are in the middle of, I understand. What I want you to know is that it doesn't matter that the husband, the brother, the father, the cousin, the friend is using different methods. What matters is that you realize their manipulation of your love does not have to be your reality. Please ask for help. There is always someone who will help you when you least expect it.

The Rant

Let's get something out of the way right at the beginning that to me the personal is the political. I, Fatemeh Shahrzad Hamzeh, a bisexual female Iranian Artist, am a political person by birth. So talking here with you is a rebellious political act against all that I have been taught as an Iranian Muslim woman.

I think, because I was born a woman, and because I was born in the Islamic Republic, I am by default a political person. Women's bodies have always been a tool for governments to use in their games of power. The fact that I am objecting here on this paper to the domestic violence I have been through is a political act. Because by the Islamic Republic's law, my husband has done nothing wrong. I am objecting to this law. I am putting what happened to me out there for others to read. I am acting against the GOVERNMENT!

I was raised to believe that talking about family problems and the shit that happened to me was a bad thing to do. I was told that everything that happened in the house or between man and wife needed to stay private. Sometimes that is true, though if my husband were beating me to death, I would like for someone to know and intervene.

That is why I am talking about this right now. Not because I need someone to intervene. As it is a matter of the past. But if I had talked about it when it was happening, someone who knew better would have slapped me out of it. If people I knew had talked about this, I probably would have known something was wrong long before things got to the point that they did.

The message I was given as a kid, teenager, and even to the early stages of adulthood, was that I talked too much, that I gave too much information away, that I needed to shut up and let people guess. The problem with this way of thinking is that by keeping quiet I will never find my own people, my community or support system.

And that was the message I kept getting from my husband. The one person that is supposed to be there for you no matter what, didn't want to hear my voice. One time I remember he had somehow gotten snow in the latch of the car door, so it would not close. He could not figure out what was wrong. As I sat in my seat, I offered some ideas to try to help solve the problem. His reaction was to yell at me that I did not actually know how things work in the world and if I could just shut up and let him think, he could figure things out a lot better.

This was one instance. There were others. Another example is when he said he wanted to come up with a game. He said that I should come up with a story, but all the stories I came up with were the wrong ones. He said I did not really understand what he meant by story. I finally realized he did not want my opinion. He wanted me to do what he wanted, when he wanted, and without asking why. He just needed someone to do his things, whatever they were, with. I was not a partner; I was not even a sidekick. I was a doll.

Sometimes I do not know when to just stay quiet. It is what he said, you know. In any situation, I just was not allowed to talk. I was there to just look pretty on his arm. Oh yes, I had to hold his arm or it meant that I did not love him. He always had a way of letting me know how I am failing at everyday life.

He would always say things like "Are you sure you want that burger? It is too expensive. Do you know how much fat is in that sandwich you are eating? You know if you get fat I might still love you, but you will no longer be pretty." And I was never allowed to respond. If I ever did react to any of the things he said, I was being too dramatic, or I was overreacting, or I was making it so that he could not say what *he* was thinking. That HE DID NOT FEEL SAFE IN OUR RELATIONSHIP.

I was a size ten when I met him. When he left I was a size 7. He kept telling me that because I do not know how to eat I am very successful at losing weight. I never really told him I wanted to lose weight. I am not sure if he knew the controversies that come with body image in performers. Did he know that as a dancer I had to put up with this bullshit literally all my life? I was always too thin for a dancer in people's eyes and I thought I passed it. I thought I had come to a country where people let you be, where people let you express yourself. I thought I had come to a free country.

I felt like I needed to slow down, ask him more questions, don't talk about myself and my life because he kept taking my words, twisting them, and using them against me in arguments. And how he kept criticizing what I ate and what I did and how I did things, even things that were not in his area of expertise. I keep thinking about how I have always been too fat or too heavy for him. And that makes me laugh because, when I did lose weight, he left... yes *he* left...

There are details to the timing and the way in which he left that I will get into, but he was the one that said he wanted to move out. Although I was the one who filed for divorce at the end.

Sometimes it seems impossible for me to find someone who would love me for me. I do not know why at that stage of my life it felt so crucial to find someone to love me. Maybe because all of my life I had to prove that I loved people, that I was worthy of love. And I got tired, you know? I wanted someone to love me without me trying to prove it, and instead I just fell into a pattern.

I think if he loved me, it would not have been so hard for him to listen to my voice. Or it would have been harder for him to insult me. He would have seen me. I did not feel seen. I felt invisible. I was just an inconvenience when he was sleeping with someone else, and I was something to fall back on when he was not sleeping with someone else.

Now, I think I have a better sense of love, I lived and learned...

I have been told repeatedly that I talk too much, that I only consider myself, and that I don't need anyone. In a weird way, now I take all those things as compliments. And maybe that is why I settled... I thought that maybe he was the last chance that I would have at finding someone to love me. Why was it so important to have someone to love me?

I remember my mom telling me that if I kept to my ways, no one would ever marry me. I think I believed my mother when she said that. And as soon as he said that he loved me, I believed him. And I held on. Maybe I did see the red flags. Maybe I knew I was ignoring the red flags. Maybe I did it intentionally, just to prove my mother's point: That though he did say he loves me, and he did marry me, but he left because I kept my ways...and in a weird way I also wanted to prove my mother wrong maybe.. Like, "See mother? I did find someone who wants to marry me." And for both reasons, I settled. I settled for the first person who seemed to want to marry me.

I think because my mother's marriage was more tolerance, than love, I followed in her footsteps. Of course, I chose my husband, and my mother was a child bride who was married off. Still, I think I was more my mother in my marriage than I care to admit. I did all that she did. I cooked, I cleaned, and I never complained. I just took it.

At the same time, I think, in my subconscious, I so badly wanted to show her that even though she never approved of me when I was growing up, I managed to do the things she said I would never be able to do.

She said that one day when she was playing by the creek in their neighborhood, her aunt showed up. She had taken my mom's hand and put a ring on it. The next thing my mom knew she was being shipped off to a new town far away from her family and friends.

I was not shipped off against my will. I chose to leave my country. Nobody forced a ring on my finger, and I thought I was in love.

The problem is, yes, I did choose my husband,but the example I had for how to treat a husband and how to be treated by a husband was far from anything that had to do with a love marriage. So of course my definition of love was distorted.

I thought I was in love. We met online, on an app called Match. He was cute. I told him I had to kiss him to know if I want to see him again; because kissing is everything.

If I don't like the way someone kisses me, I don't think I can even get wet (let alone have a whole life and family with them). This part I did not share with him!

A lot of the time, I think, I look back at my life as a 20 something year old in Iran who was not allowed to have sex, and I wonder if the fact that I was so horny made the logical part of my brain shut down 'cause he was a good kisser. I was simply too horny at the moment, and by the time I realized I had made a mistake I was in way too deep.

We kissed in his car; after we had tea in a small coffee shop on Main Street. He kissed okay. I wanted to kiss him more, but I had to go to school. I told him he could come see the play. It was my first semester and I was hosting a play for the school. I was not really a part of the production, but because the writer was Iranian, the professor who had arranged the play thought it would be good to have me welcome the audience. The show only had one actor, so I was only welcoming the audience and handing the actor the script. the actor was not supposed to see it before the show.

He came to the show. I saved him a seat. He asked to cook me dinner after. I said I would love that. We did not eat. Instead, He kissed me and made me promise to see him again. Then we slept together. I did not cum.

I did not trust him enough. I don't think I ever fully trusted him. And that makes me sad sometimes... that I knew deep down that he is not to be trusted, but I ignored my gut feelings because he seemed affectionate.

He kept trying to convince me that condoms are a bad idea. You see a person who has seen healthy relationships would have known this is a red flag. However, I did not see the red flag. I saw a guy who seemed to like me. I showered. He washed my underwear for me when I said I wish I had clean underwear.

That night we did use a condom, but a couple of weeks later we talked to a Dr. so I could go on birth control. Now that I look back, it feels like I had to pay the price for his lifestyle. If one does not like condoms then they should be the one taking precautions, like he could have had a vasectomy. But when I brought it up he said he needed his balls!!! That was a really bullshit answer especially for someone who is a doctor. I did not question it though, I do not think at the time I was thinking quite rationally.

His parents visited him the next day, but we saw each other every day for the rest of that week. He would even go to school with me and wait for dance rehearsals to end. He picked me up. He dropped me off. He took care of me. He was literally there all the time, like he was watching my every move.

Now that I look back, I would say that's also a red flag. He did not trust me enough to be where I said I would be, or that I would get to our date on time. Or that I would still exist maybe... I do not know.

But I loved it. I loved that this other person, this man, was so interested in me. He would do anything I asked and tell me nice things. He was making me feel like I really had someone who truly loved me. And maybe in my subconscious I was telling my mother, "See mother? I did it... I found me a man who likes my ways..."

In my mother's family, a lot of the time, people do not treat you like a human being if you are not married. Like you do not get tired, or you have no purpose. My mom, sometimes, when she was delivering the news of someone getting married in her family would sound so sad. She would say: "God willing, one day my daughters too will get married."

The getting married was important, not to whom, not the connection, and certainly not the love, as long as the person you were marrying had a good job, had a car, and a house. I wonder if I married for my mother... of course I am a grown ass woman, and I did make choices. I think, to have just come out of an oppressive environment where I was taught to willingly give up my anatomy, it was a bit hard for me to separate my own feelings from the feelings of those I love.

Speaking of doing things others want, I later also realized that I was not sure if I wanted to have sex with him on that first night. I just did it. I thought I was supposed to. I had to show him I could do what he wanted. He wanted to have sex. And I had sex with him. I just did not know how to say no. And of course he later used this against me.

I later found out he was a sex addict, and he liked to have sex only under his conditions. I could not criticize or give feedback. I could not tell him what I liked, and I certainly could not say no. Whenever I refused to have sex with him, he would deprive me of any sort of touch for months at a time. I was dying a bit every day, as I love to be touched, even if it is just a caress.

Sometimes just so he would touch me, I would let him pick at my skin. He would tell me that I have these weird spots on my skin, especially on my arms, and that they look like pimples. So he would try to pop them. He would press my skin so it would start bleeding. I would have scabs for days. I never asked him to stop. I so badly needed someone, anyone, in any form, to touch me.

I was so thirsty for touch, I was literally going crazy. Add that on top of the fact that I had no one to talk to... I would catch myself talking to my stuffed animals or myself about my daily life. It had made it so that sometimes I would forget other people existed, and I would blurt out whatever I was thinking.

He asked me to marry him two months in, and I said yes; because we were in love, and it was magical. Of course I said yes! All I could think at the time was that why else would you want to date someone? If you want to marry them and you know it, what is the point of waiting? If you want to live with them in the same house you have to be married. Now that I look back I realize that might be why he asked me to marry him, because I told him I cannot tell my mother I am living with a man I am not married to. I would have dated him for years, but I would not have moved in with him with the mindset that I had at the time.

So yes, I said yes to his proposal because I wanted to live with the man I thought I loved. I wanted to be with him, and I wanted it to last forever. I wanted it to be permanent, and I thought, that way, it would be harder for his ex-wife to seduce him... Again...

Yes, there was an ex-wife who kept calling when we were together, and he said that she was crazy. What I missed about the situation was that there were choices being made on his part. There were many moments where he could have ended everything with her, but he did not want to.

He said he did not block her because he used to hit her, and she was threatening to sue. So, he talked to her sometimes. But he loved me and wanted to marry me. An experienced logical person would have seen this as a very red flag. This was a bloody flag. This man is admitting to having been violent with his ex-wife. This was bad.

In my 24 year old mind though, I rationalized it that *I* was different. He *loved* me. He would *never* hurt me. Especially the way he narrated the story, it sounded like she had personally uttered the words "choke me till I pass out". He said she had episodes where she would go nuts and start smashing everything; that is why she had asked him to choke her to near death so she would stop, even if for a minute.

This was very bad! Why did I stay silent? Why did I continue to see him? Do I not call myself a feminist? I ask myself sometimes how I could have stood up for him. Was it so important to have someone to "love" me that I ignored his violent past? What is love? How do I define it that having someone violent love me is worth the lost integrity?

I think I am, and I got, angry at myself more than I was, and I am, and I got, mad at him or the relationship. I should have known better. I have traveled. I have read. I now have about 12 years of college under my belt. Is having the wrong role model this formative on an impressionable young mind that all the things I know to be wrong seemed okay when they were happening to me?

What I did not know at the time was that she was not an ex-wife. She was his wife. They were still married when he proposed to me. I was the other woman. She had every right to call him. She had every right. Period. It was easy to believe him. He lived alone. And *I was in love.*

The only reason he even told me that there is an "ex-wife" was because we were going to meet his parents, and he was afraid they would tell me. So, he decided to tell me there was an "ex-wife"; an insane one. Someone he had divorced a few months before he met me. One that tortured him and had no regard for his "allergies".

Yes, he had allergies. He was basically allergic to anything and everything that brought me joy. His "allergies" were a tool for him to control me and what was inside the house. Let me give you an example. I have a dream to have a library of my own, something like what you might have seen in *Downton Abbey.* Some of my friends know this, so if they have books they think I would like, they give the books to me. A friend of mine gave me a few books and I had them in my closet.

The books were there for a couple of weeks when my husband decided to vacuum the house. While vacuuming, he stepped into my closet and saw the books. Within the hour, he got "sick" and he knew exactly what he was "allergic" to. He very angrily asked me to get rid of the books. I did get rid of some of them, but I moved a few of them to the outer bookshelf in my room. At this point, I knew he only wanted to hurt and control me, and I was learning how to go around him. As soon as he looked in the closet and saw the books "gone", he was all better!

Of course, I did not see it that way when he first brought it up. He politely asked me to stop wearing my perfume. I did. Can you imagine a Persian not wearing perfume? (I think it is necessary to mention that Persians love their perfume. They basically drown themselves in perfume when they are going out.) But I was in love or so I thought; I would have done anything for him. And I did. I did everything and anything he asked. And he kept asking for more. It was never enough. I was never enough. I would never be enough.

At first the things he asked me to stop doing were small things. They were few and far between. As days and weeks passed, the things he was allergic to seemed to grow more in number. And then I realized there was a theme. All of these things are things that I have either expressed some joy for, or I was the one who had brought them in the house.

There was a part of him that was erasing my heritage. Before we got married, my sister, who had immigrated to the USA a few months before me, decided to visit Iran. When she came back she had brought me some *Namad*[1] table cloth from southern Iran. She had also brought me one of her *Geleems*[2] that she had made during her undergrad. He said he was allergic to their presence in the house even if I put them in a suitcase in the basement. So, I gave them to my brother. I think that really hurt my sister. Not because I gave them to my brother but because it seemed I had no regard for the trouble she had gone to, to bring a piece of our culture into my new home.

And despite all the changes I made, he still wasn't happy. I think if I had died, it would have made him happy. That might have been the thing that could make him happy. He was never happy. I was being oppressed on a daily basis. In a way I had my very own personal Islamic Republic!

I find it particularly interesting that I had traveled literally half way across the world to avoid marrying a man who was raised with that thought structure and in that environment, and I had managed to find a white man who was very similar in thought process to those of the Taliban and devotees of the Islamic Republic.

I tolerated, and I tolerated. Did the behavior he showed seem normal? I cannot remember a happy couple I had seen. All my high school friends who had gotten married, they all hated their husbands, at least that's what they told me.

The things they, my highschool friends and classmates, said about how they were not allowed to do certain things. They could not and cannot report their husbands or get a divorce because of the country that we live in--well, they live in. I left...

They all had to put up with it, especially because most of them had kids. If they had gotten a divorce, they would not have gotten custody. They might never have seen their children again. In my head I used to say that I would never be in *that* situation. And here I was acting like what I had witnessed all my life.

I kept asking myself : "is this what it is to be married? Is this a husband?" for it was all I had seen throughout my life. I had judged it, I had wondered. And there I was in the middle of something I had thought unfair when it was happening to others. I could understand that people I grew up with did not have choices, but I was in America! How did this happen? I ask myself, and I know that I should not be blaming myself, and yet ...

When I look back I realize I did not know I could leave. I wanted to. What I did was I would volunteer for everything. I was always somehow busy creating something new. I would try to take on all the projects that I could. Somehow I was very productive in my very stressful life, kind of like stress was my drug of choice.

Sometimes it felt like I was too hungry for his attention that I would take anything he would throw at me, even if it was an insult. I was lonely. I really wanted him to be there for me and he just could not. All he could offer was the way he saw the things

I did. He saw all that I was doing *wrong*, if there is even such a concept when it comes to life.

He kept criticizing my outfits. He kept telling me things like, "People don't wear stuff like that here." Or that "your pants are too tight" Or that "you do not actually know how to dress". He would suggest for us to just stay in...There was always something wrong with what I wore in his eyes. He kept saying that because I am from a different culture I do not understand how people dress here. Sometimes I wonder how I could have put up with all of that, and I realize that I was prepared for it.

I was trained to tolerate such behavior. I was born a woman in the Islamic Republic of Iran who had been trained to keep silent against violence done to her. They treat you like shit in the Islamic Republic. They tell you what to wear and how to wear it, and then they tell you that it is out of love. They tell you that if they did not love you they would not have tortured you for the "wrongs" that you did[3].

Ordinary people, who you don't even know, in the streets comment on your appearance and outfit, sometimes a random guy on a motorcycle even gives himself the permission to spank you because your butt was just asking for it.

I sometimes think I even expected it. I expected my husband to be horrible to me. Because where I grew up violence against women is normal. It is normal to tell women that they do not understand. It is normal for husbands to beat the shit out of their wives and for wives to just get used to it. That is what husbands do, is it not? They hurt you... at least that was what I had witnessed all around me as a child, teenager, and adult.

Eventually, I realized his criticism was born out of his desire to fight. He did not know how to be happy. He wanted me to disagree with him and put up some sort of a resistance to his illogical requests. But I do not like fighting. I wanted to avoid being yelled at, and he just could not help it. HE HAD TO YELL! Because I simply "DID NOT UNDERSTAND!" I was just "a stupid idiot".

I look back and I get a mixed rush of emotions. I feel angry that I did all of that knowing I deserved better. I feel sympathy for my younger self who was looking for love. I feel sad that I had no one to talk to. Not really. Everybody wanted to give advice. I wanted someone to listen.

I was confused most of the time. He would ask me to shut up and not say anything. Then he would ask me random questions and if I did not answer, he would yell at me for being an "asshole mute." I was always doing everything wrong.

He would ask me to go shopping for groceries and start cooking at home, then when I had the food ready he would say he feels like going out so we are going out. He was mostly contradicting himself and when I would try to confront him he would say that I was making things up. I tried recording our conversations, So, that I could go back to it. I swear it was like he knew. He would sit by me on the sofa and stay silent for hours even when I would try to strike up a conversation.

There was always something that was making him physically sick or upset. I just did not realize it until after we got married. I moved in with him a week before the wedding. He said he would take me on a trip if I didn't invite anyone to the wedding. I did not invite any of my friends to the wedding. And there was no dancing, because he did not like parties. This was a huge sacrifice for me because I am a dancer.

Dancing is a big part of who I am. That is *THE REASON* why I left my home country, because dancing is illegal in Iran. So not dancing at my own wedding was a huge sacrifice, especially since I did not have my family here. They were across the world from me. But I loved him. And in love you make sacrifices. You compromise. You make it work. You meet each other in the middle. I do not know if there was a middle between my husband and I. It was all his territory and I was intruding.

When I decided not to have a party for my wedding, I wasn't unhappy with the decision. I was content. In my 24 year old mind and body I thought that these kinds of decisions are ones you make when you get married and have a husband. You sacrifice. I might have taken it too far, as I completely forgot to consider my own needs. That is what he did. He chose himself and his own comfort and he pushed for it. I gave in. I did not present my case. And the way he presented it, it was so we could have a bigger budget for a trip after the wedding as a long weekend was coming up.

Later on he said that there was no budget and there would be no trip. "As we are already married and there's no need to spend money we do not have on a trip we can take in the coming months and over a longer holiday or vacation".

I was happy that day. I was marrying who I thought was the love of my life. I thought I was going on a trip right after and that really was what I wanted at that moment. I do not regret the decision. What makes me mad at myself is that I believed him even though he kept promising me things that he had no intention of living up to.

We got married in a court. No photographers. He said he couldn't take the stress of a wedding and posing for a photographer on the same day. He later blamed my lack of readiness for the wedding day. It took me a while to realize it was always going to be my fault in my so-called "love marriage." We had lunch with his parents at a restaurant in town after the "wedding". The waiter brought us a cupcake with a candle on it for dessert. That made my day.

His parents followed us home after the wedding lunch. We talked, and his mom told me how she did not like the idea of her son marrying so soon after his divorce. She was right. He should not have gotten married a couple of months after his first divorce. I found this fact out way after our wedding that his divorce was finalized right before our wedding. His ex-wife sent me a picture of the divorce decree later on.

I still tried to defend him to his ex-wife. When she kept telling me that he was a liar and a cheater, I kept saying that he would never lie to me. She laughed at me. I was so young. I was so in love. I thought about having kids. We did not have kids. I am happy about that, even though that is why I started looking for a partner.

I had this irrational fear that my parents are going to die any minute, and I needed my kids to know them. I love my parents, but I am happy I did not have kids with him. He would have made a horrible father. I said that to him. Closer to the end, I said he did not deserve to be a father. I believed that, because he treated me horribly and I knew something was wrong. I needed this cycle to be broken. I think one day I will fully forgive myself for staying as long as I did because I needed time to unlearn all the oppression I had been through. But if there were kids involved in this situation, I do not think I would ever be able to forgive myself for putting them in a situation I could have chosen not to bring them into.

Sometimes when I think back, I realize I have had many chances to walk out the door. But I stayed. Because I did not know any better. And when you are treated that way over time it becomes your reality.

... and maybe I should have known better. There was the moment where I realized even after marrying me; he was still carrying on a relationship with his ex wife. There was the time when I found out he was still on match.com, or the time when

I realized he was on tinder, or when he kicked me out of the house, or any of the times he called me an idiot and questioned my intelligence.

My mom once told me a woman has to love her husband. I love my mom. I do. And in a way she was right. You are supposed to love your spouse. I also think hearing what she said as a ten year old might have done some damage, though. Now, I know. I know I need to love myself and men can fuck off if they don't appreciate me. But I was in love, and I lost myself. I chipped away little pieces of myself in hopes that he would love me. Or maybe I wanted to be worthy of his love.

But he would never love me. Sometimes I thought he was not capable of love. He once looked me in the eye and said: "You are way out of my league, you are going to leave me one day anyway. So, what is the point?"

And maybe that is why he was so horrible to me. He was trying to see what would push me over the edge. What would make me *leave* him...? Do not get me wrong. I understand that I made mistakes. Of course I did. I was a fucking kid. I did not defend myself when he started attacking me. I did not defend my culture when he started attacking it. I did not defend my family when he started trash talking. I did not defend my position as a spouse.

Mostly I was scared. I think. Every time he yelled I backed away a little bit till there was nothing left. I did not trust him one tiny bit. I felt out of place for feeling distrust towards him.

It felt wrong to be in the same space with him. I wondered if this is it. This is what it is to be married. As I had heard people tell me that I should not get married. That is the way to live... single... men will just ruin it all...

The first time I found out he was on a dating app I thought nothing of it. It was maybe three months or less into our marriage. My sister texted me asking: "Why is your husband still on this dating app?" She was single at the time and she had found his profile. I confronted him. He said he talked to his friends who were on the app. He deleted the app in front of me. He hugged me, and went quiet for a few minutes. Like a child when he knows he has done something wrong.

I let it go. I did not ask why your friends are on a dating app. I did not ask my sister to take screenshots. I did not ask to see his chats or the app. I let it go; maybe because I was not ready to face the reality of him. That he lied, and that he needed to be on those apps, not only because he had a problem with commitment, but because he believed there must be something wrong with me to have loved and married him.

Time passed. At some point I realized he was talking to his ex-wife. And of course they were fucking in my bed, my bed, my queen size bed with the wooden headboard, and its firm mattress. I always slept on the left side of the bed, with him on my right side. But I believed him when he said, "It is just texting". I later sold the bed for $250.

His ex-wife lost it at some point. She would not stop calling him. She would not stop calling me. She would steal our mail. She would sit in her car outside our door waiting for him to go out or come home. She would leave comments on his mother's and my sister's Instagram page talking about what a cheater he is.

I had to call the police. It was becoming too much. But that is when I realized he did not know how to, or maybe did not want to, be there for me. Her friends were texting me that I should go away so she and my husband can be together again. He showed me some of the texts they had sent him. That I am some random girl and he should be with the love of his life.

I wonder why he showed me those texts, you know? Did he want me to think he was choosing me? Did he want me to have the illusion of an honest husband? Was it part of a bigger plan? Was he trying to get me to a high where he was the man of my dreams? To then drop me down to prove to me that he has power over me? That he is the only person who can get me to that high again? Why did he show me those messages? Did he want a trophy? Was he pretending to be transparent? Was it part of a bigger plan?

I asked him what he was going to do about this situation, and he said: "Nothing". When I think about it, I realize that he might have enjoyed the situation. He was getting all this attention, and it looked like two women were fighting over him.

I do not know. All I know is that that whole situation was when my crazy in love marriage started to look like a prison.

I wanted my man to be there for me, to be the man who showed me the texts. I wanted him to support me. I wanted him to put a stop to the emotional torture that I was being targeted for. Perhaps I expected too much of a man who had by then already cheated on me multiple times. At the time though, it did not seem like too much to ask of my husband. Someone who I thought was my partner in life.

Yes, he was difficult. It was not the first time I had realized that I am not his entire world. But I still did not realize I was not even in his world. I noticed he was conveniently allergic to all of my stuff, and anything I had a desire for. But I was happy to not have anything. Because I thought I had him. I did not have him. His previous relationship was not over yet. I had interrupted it unknowingly.

When he said he did not care that all of these random people were texting me and telling me all these horrible things, something broke. I started to get defensive. I realized what my grandmother meant when she said, "You should not show all of yourself to your husband." I started having all these little secrets, which were not really secrets. I just did not want to tell him everything anymore.

At first, it was just hiding a few dollars in a shoe box. I later realized he had found the box. He went through my stuff. I could not hide things. I would like to think my home was a safe place, but apparently it was not as he enjoyed going through my closet and other spaces.

During the lockdown I tried to kill myself again and again…His response at the time was that he would help me move out. He did not ask why. He did not try to find a solution for my deepest sorrow. He simply asked me to leave. It appears I loved a shadow. I loved someone who was not even there. I loved the idea of a love marriage. But I was not loved.

And when I look at the whole pandemic thing, I wondered why he never got COVID. He showed extreme sensitivity to even a trace of dust in my closet, causing him to fall ill for days until I complied with his requests. Despite this, he came into direct contact with individuals infected with COVID-19 without experiencing any illness?

I remember catching myself wishing he would get COVID and die. I so desperately wanted to become a widow of the virus. Sometimes I feel ashamed for wanting another human dead. But I did… I would fantasize about getting a call from a random hospital in the middle of nowhere telling me my husband had been in an accident and they wanted me to come down and identify the body…

I talk too much. I am talking too much. I am telling you that I fantasized about my husband's death…You see, I did not get a chance to talk when I was in my "prison". Talking feels liberating. I enjoy letting it all out, especially because we do not know each other. I am telling you because I believe if I had heard others talk about what they went through, I would have tried to leave sooner...

At some point during the pandemic he said he is getting allergic to the mask, so he made me change the bed covers every day and wash them. I was not sure what the allergy was because I wasn't seeing anything on his face. I just knew if I do not change the covers I will be accused of not caring about him and being selfish. So, I kept changing the covers from the white ones to the ones with the blue flowers and I washed them every day. I do not remember when he decided it was okay to go back to washing the sheets on a weekly basis.

It took me so long to realize I needed to leave. I did not know any better. Yes, I am mad at myself for loving who I loved. Do not get me wrong, I do not regret my marriage, and I do not regret my divorce. I am better for it. What I am saying is that my experience might help someone out there, and maybe all this does not have to happen to someone else... Maybe my entire trauma happened for a reason. Maybe...

I think it was about a week into our marriage that I found him crying while playing video games. I asked him what was wrong and he started yelling at me. He said that he was too tired of my inquiries and I should just let him calm down when he comes home from work.

I went to the other bedroom. I remember asking myself if I made a mistake. He came after me. I wiped my tears as I did not want him to see my tears. He wanted dinner and he was mad that there was no food in the house. He then left the house without saying anything. He was gone for hours.

This disappearance was a recurring event. He never felt like he owed me any explanation. If I ever asked he would make it look like I am a controlling wife who is always just too thirsty for attention. Maybe I was thirsty for attention, controlling though, I never really had the energy to be.

I remember one time I was trying to understand his sadness. He was being an asshole. I tried to cheer him up and get him to get off his computer. Yes, I wanted attention from my husband. All he had to say were hurtful things that would make me cry. He would not get up to console me, and I thought to myself that "it's okay! My husband is having a bad day!" So, I would leave the room and try to calm myself down. I would come back and try again maybe three times? I want it to be three times though I know it was two times. He told me that I was mentally unstable because I cried and smiled within the same half hour.

One time when I came out of the shower I found him lying on the ground staring into the abyss. And since I had not yet learned my lesson, I asked him what was wrong. He started telling me about how he was a horrible husband and that is why his ex wife left him, and if he was a better man she would have stayed.

At this point in the marriage I still did not know the whole story. What he had told me was that she left him for another man. So, keep in mind that I still had not seen the divorce decree or realized his "crazy" ex was telling the truth. What he had told me was what I believed to be true.

So, as naïve as I was, I told him that that may be true. But he has a new wife now and he should care for her. Unless he wants the new wife to also realize he is a bad husband and leave. And he cried. He cried very hard and long and said that he does not want that. He said that he knows he has to take care of our marriage.

He did become more attentive. He would tell me that he is going out and when he is coming back. I trusted him. To love is to trust. It turns out all this while he was still having relations with his ex wife, and all of this was to distract me from whatever it was that was happening behind my back.

It did not take long though, not even a month. And he was mean again. He was angry. He was tired as soon as I wanted to do something. I remember begging him to go to the movies with me. He said the movies was a stupid place to go in this time and age when we could watch it all at home in the comfort of our bed. I am not sure why I felt guilty to go alone... I should have gone to the movies on my own. I had money. I had a car. I was a grown ass woman.

I think perhaps it was the fact that I wanted to have the experience with my husband, Or maybe to show the world that I have a man on my arm. Perhaps I just wanted to go to the movies with my husband. Sometimes I look back and judge myself. Even though I know when those things happened, and when

I made those decisions I must have felt like there was no other choice.

Sometimes he would ask me to wait for him to eat. He would ask me to cook. So, when he comes home from work he can have a warm homemade meal and we can eat together like the in-love couple that we are. He worked all over Illinois. Sometimes by the time he would get home it would be ten at night. He would get home. I would be there in the kitchen almost done with putting the meal together, and he would tell me that he has already eaten.

"Why did you ask me to cook then?" "I got too hungry by the time I was done." "Text me next time? So, I can eat?" "Sure." And he would never text me. He kept doing this. He kept making me cook and wait, and he kept promising to let me know the next time. He never did. Why did I keep falling for it?

I loved him. I did. I loved him so much. I counted the seconds every day to see him again, even when he was mean to me. I would literally feel him come home. I would open the door before he had put the key in lock. He called me a witch. For sensing him, and for all the herbs I had. I had an herb for every pain and sore. I am Persian after all.

I waited patiently to greet him every single day, of course that was before completely losing faith in my choice of a husband. He got meaner every day, though. At some point it got really difficult to talk to him.

Sometimes he would tell me that because I have an accent he has difficulty understanding me, and I best not say anything. He said that my English was not good enough for conversation.

Oftentimes, He would get mad and yell at me for no reason at all. Was it love I wonder... is love supposed to feel like a prison? Is it supposed to hurt so much on the inside that you grow a desire to physically hurt yourself? Why was he so mean and angry all the time? He would call me an idiot for sport at least three times a week.

And I felt like an idiot... for loving him. I have an entry in one of my journals that I am copying here for you:

"I am sad. I am upset. I am a lot of things. I really really hate him. I hate myself for listening to him and giving in. I hate myself for not fighting for my rights, for what is truly what I deserve and I should have. I give up and I give in because I need it to be over, I need everyone to be happy, and that is why I just say okay and agree to everything because I just need them to stop yelling at me. I feel like my opinion does not matter in this relationship, which of course is not a new thing. I do not know why it surprises me every time he does something that makes it clear that he does not care for me or about me.

"I felt abandoned. I felt used. I felt like my marriage was doomed. Any day now, I'll realize that I am better off with someone else. Something I already know deep down but I keep hoping. I am in love with the idea of love. But am I really truly in love with this man who expected me to just live in a dungeon?

"*Before signing the lease, my brother and I went and looked at the apartment for my husband and me. My brother told me that, from the looks of the place, it was not a very good place. I told that to my husband, but he went on with leasing the place anyway.*

"*A Couple of days ago, I went to get the keys. They would not give me the keys unless I signed a bunch of stuff and gave them the rent for the first month. When my brother and I went inside the apartment, I was petrified. I could not believe my husband had agreed to pay $1750 for this place. It was such a small place. The ceiling was really low and the walls felt too close to each other. The stairs were too shallow and they were hard to climb. The house smelled like it was just painted but not a clean paint. The walls had cracks in them and it looked like there was water damage going on all over the apartment. The bedrooms were too small. I do not think our king size bed would fit in any of them. There was no washer and dryer in the apartment, though they had shown us pictures of an apartment with washer and dryer. I felt overwhelmed. I could not breathe and I needed to throw up.*

"*I looked at the apartment, and the first thing that came to my mind was that I cannot bring anyone over. It looked abandoned. I felt like my husband should have been ashamed of wanting me to live here. The reason we ended up with this place was because he said the apartment at my brother's place was too expensive. I did not think so. But He did not listen to me. He just did what he wanted, and I did not fight for what I knew to be right at the time.*

"I was devastated. I do not know what to do. I talked to a couple of friends, and they said some good things. They said that I was not stuck in the lease and that I didn't really have to live there if I did not want to. I returned the keys the day after, after taking pictures of every corner of the apartment and the outside of it. That horrible place will haunt me to my grave.

"That memory might fade, but I will not forget the feelings I went through all day. I felt helpless, and alone. I should not have felt like that. I should have a husband who can make me feel safe. Why can't my husband do that? Why am I afraid of my husband? Why does it feel like I have to be careful and not make any mistakes or he won't love me anymore? Why do I have to apologize for being who I am, and what I want? AM I ASKING TOO MUCH?

"How do I explain what I went through today? How do I describe it to do it justice? How can I bring it on paper so I will remember and never forget? How do I take lessons from this, and not let this kind of thing happen again?"

I remember that day, and I remember feeling helpless... And I am glad I wrote it down. I do still wonder if a marriage should feel like a prison... if it should feel like a rollercoaster. I had to be very careful about every word that came out of my mouth because I was not safe in the presence of my husband.

We ended up getting an apartment at the complex where my brother lived. But boy did my husband make sure it was hell. He kept saying he is allergic to the apartment. And since he was allergic to it, he would make me clean it. As you must guess, of course I cleaned it in a way that made him even more allergic.

We could have gotten a three-bedroom for $2000 a month when we first got a quote. He refused to sign the lease for that one, and we ended up paying $2400 for a two-bedroom on the first floor when we finally signed a lease with them a few months later.

He brought our stuff in a truck on September 20th 2021 from Bloomington, IL to Richardson, TX. I was staying with my brother from August 10th because I needed to do stuff for school. Yes, I applied to UT Dallas because of my brother; because my brother was living in Dallas, and I needed to be around family.

When my husband got here, I remember being excited to see him. But he started cursing at me because he was unhappy driving a big truck. I remember feeling heartbroken. Yet, I slept with him that night. Again, not because I longed for him, but because that is what you do when you haven't seen your lover for a long time.

I remember we had sex on the couch. He was sitting on the loveseat. He did not take his clothes off; I had just come out of the shower. He told me I have become really tiny. He laughed. He looked exhausted, because he had tried to set everything up before he had to leave. He came on a Friday, but he left on a Monday because he was not certified to work in Texas yet.

It did not matter that I told him I was going to Dallas, even before applying to UT Dallas. He didn't believe that I was good enough to get into a PhD program. He said that we better buy a house and start having kids.... "You have the hips, why not use them?" is what he told me. He said his family was depending on him to carry on the family name and bloodline since his sister could not have kids.

So, he mocked me and refused to get certified to work in Texas. It took him until Thanksgiving that year to fully join me. And since I had not packed everything for him to bring, he had thrown away half our stuff...

I later found out that while I was in Texas, he was having an affair with someone. Surprise, surprise. I think I expected it though... you know? He did not understand intimacy. All he understood was sex. I used to read to him every night before bed. Even when I was away on a trip, I read to him over the phone... I wrote him letters every single day when I was in some place that he wasn't.

I know that I did those things not just because I was trying to be close to my husband, but also for me. I loved doing all those things. And I will keep being proud of the experiences I gave him. I hope that the next woman will have it just a little bit better if she ever finds herself in his clutches, as his experiences with me have helped him become a better man. Or so I hope...

I did all those things because I was trying to be with my husband even though I was not physically there. I was being romantic. I was trying to let him know that I am here, and that he is not alone. Yet, he justified his unfaithfulness by saying that he was lonely. I think it was because our definitions of love and intimacy were different.

It is okay to have different definitions as long as you are forward with them. We even had different definitions of cheating. Sometimes I think I could have gotten past all the cheating if he had been honest about it. I even once told him that whatever he does he should never lie to me because that is the one thing I can never stand for or get over. I cannot take being lied to. And he just could not help himself.

We went to couple's counseling, you know? It was after he beat me and kicked me out of the house. It was the first fall during COVID. It was September, and he was mad because I asked him to explain something for the third time. Or the second time? I want it to be the third time because I still cannot believe he got so mad... he called me a stupid idiot, and when I ran and slammed the door, he ran after me. He broke the door, pulled me by the arm, and then shoved me to the stairs. Sometimes I still feel an excruciating pain in my arm when I write for a few minutes.

He said, "get out of here you stupid little shit" and shoved me one more time. I almost fell down the stairs, but I held myself up. I took my laptop, my camera, and a couple of books, and left. I did not go to my sister's house... I should have... and here is why I feel like an idiot...I did not want my sister to think my husband was a bad person. Why? I still do not understand the logic behind my idiocy...

But it might have something to do with the examples that were set for me. I remember my dad saying, "Whatever happens in between these four walls shall never leave these four walls". And by "these four walls" he meant our house. Talking about what went on in your house was just something you do not do. People should not know what happens to you, even getting beaten to death.

I love my dad. I would die for my dad. Of course, he and the way he thinks have changed over the years. I understand, and at the time he might have been right because we lived in a dictatorship. There were and are spies everywhere. No one knew who to trust.

When things are taken out of context sometimes they make no sense. Like the example with my dad. He was raising daughters in an Islamic Dictatorship. And to a younger and older version of me being with my husband will never make sense. It made sense for the 24 year old me who had just left a country in which she could not report rape. I was happy to have found him. He too was or at least seemed happy...

Anyway...

I did not go to my sister's house. If I had, she or her boyfriend would have made me call the police. And I should have called the police but I did not. I was so afraid of everything. I thought if no one knew I could make it better, and when he is the perfect husband I can present him ... see? I was a kid...

I started calling women's shelters hoping one of them would take me in. None did... They wanted me to wait in line for over a week, and I just needed a place to sleep that night. I look back now and see myself sitting in my car in the garage, hoping some lightning would strike me... I wanted to die...

I kept asking myself, "How could I have let this happen? Why am I in this situation?" I felt like it was all me, and I realized how grateful I was for taking birth control.

If there had been a kid in this situation, I think I would have had a harder time forgiving myself. Not only for putting myself in this awful situation, but for being responsible for another being's hardship, and setting an example of such behavior for them.

I kept calling shelter after shelter and one of them mentioned they could give me money to go to a hotel. And that gave me an idea.... I remembered I have a credit card! It was his, but I did have "money".

I checked into a hotel not very far from our townhouse. He called me a few times, and then he gave up. He sent some texts about how I should not have pissed him off and that I can go back now. I ignored him. I showered. I threw what I was wearing in the trash can. I watched a movie, and I went to bed.

Before I came to the US, I had this habit of running away from reality by watching a show. Sometimes I even would stay up three days in a row just to live in that world. Believe it or not, I could still function in everyday life. I would get things done and go back to my alternate reality.

But When I came to the US, the need to run away went away. I could feel that in this society, I was more accepted even though I was not everyone's cup of tea. I wanted to get better at being myself every day, and I did.

When I was kicked out of my home by my husband, that need to get away came back. My reality hurt too much to live in it...

I also started dancing more and more to get away, because that is what I do. I use my dancing to be myself away from others. In a way, I was being my best self while I was being abused... that is a sad way to look at it. Did I have Stockholm syndrome? Abuse is what I have known all my life, not only because of the horrible romantic partners that I have had, but also in relation to the society and the community I was a part of as an Iranian woman.

To grow out of that society I had to ignore all the abuse and sometimes pretend that nothing has happened. If I had started processing, I would have stopped functioning. And to keep going in an environment like that conditions your mind and body, you know? The rollercoaster is all I had ever known...

It took me two months, but I reported him to the police. It was October 2020 when I called the non emergency line at Bloomington Police department. An officer came to talk to me. When I was talking to him I started crying. He was an older man, tall, big belly, and two of his fingers on his left hand were chopped off. He looked at me and he said: "you know you should leave him. Right? Because it is a cycle... He is never going to be the man you want him to be. You are young. Just leave him. I am sure you will find someone who will treat you right."

I am not sure why the incident I am about to tell you made me want to report him, but something clicked in my mind. Like, wake up Shah... he is not a good man! I was in the kitchen, and his phone was charging on the counter. And I think I wanted to check something on the web and I did not have my phone with me. I opened his phone, and there it was: Tinder, open on the messaging section. He had a lady-in-waiting in every little town in Illinois. I remember waiting for him to fall asleep that night, coming down, and taking pictures with my phone of every single message he had exchanged. And boy there was no end.

The hardest part of COVID for me was that I was stuck at home with my husband. And I was getting to *really know* him... I mean I knew he was a liar, I just did not know the degree to which he would twist shit when it was coming out of his mouth.

I think that is when I stopped wearing my wedding ring...

And it is amazing how he pretended like he never lies. To the point when I asked him to ask my sister to come over for dinner so that we could surprise her for her birthday he said that he could not lie! What I asked him to do was not exactly a lie. There would have been dinner served.

My sister's boyfriend was trying to surprise her for her birthday and it was supposed to happen in our townhouse. There were guests. There was dinner. My husband, though, decided to have dinner on his own without telling me or anyone else. Even though he knew we would be waiting for him to join us.

A whole party of people was waiting for him. He had known and promised to be there by five thirty, and he showed up at seven, having already eaten. He then kept asking when the party was going to leave.

What makes me even sadder is that my sister's boyfriend had also put my name on the cake. In his mind, my husband would have asked him to make this a double party as my sister's and my birthday are a day apart. It was a very considerate act on my sister's boyfriend's part, but it seems he overestimated my husband's affection for me. My husband did not even get me a birthday present that year.

I told his mom about the Tinder, I texted her that he is cheating on me, and I asked her not to tell him because he does not know that I know. Why tell his mom? I sometimes ask myself. What did I have to gain? How would she be able to help me? Because I just needed to tell someone or maybe because I was trying to prove to her that there is something wrong with her son.

She had a theory on why I was marrying her son, and the theory was that I just wanted a husband, and he was in a vulnerable state so I was taking advantage. The idea that maybe I just loved her son seemed a little too hard for her to believe, I guess. I have no idea why she was convinced that I was going to leave him by the first spring after our wedding.

I think a part of me wanted her to know that even if I did leave (you see at this point I still was not sure I was leaving, I was that naïve that he would become the man I actually met) I would be leaving because he is a horrible man, not because I am a bad wife who does not know how to keep her husband in check.

The interesting thing about the situation (or anything that ever happened in my marriage and I told his mom about) is that she never told the dad. She said that these things made him upset. And I should also stop texting in the group chat about whatever is upsetting because he does not want the image of his son ruined.

It was then when I realized he has never faced consequences for anything that he has done. He always seemed so oblivious to the idea of consequence. The fact that the nature of his relationship with his ex wife was still the same as when they were married is another example of why he did not seem to understand that once I leave I am truly gone.

Consequences made no sense to him. It was a foreign concept to my educated husband, which is why I think his reaction to me calling the cops was more like "you made a mistake Shahrzad" rather than "oh, I fucked up!"

I called his mom the same day I called the police. After the Police left I was scared to death because the officer said he had to talk to my husband. I actually started sweating on an October day in Illinois. I panicked. I told him I wanted to take it all back, and he said that his camera was on and he recorded everything.

He said he had to hear my husband's side as well. He said that he would come back to talk to my husband. I was so scared. I called my sister and I asked her to please come over. She said that they were going to come over that night and I could talk to her when she gets there. I said that I was scared and I needed to see her.

She came over. I told her about the cop and told her about telling my husband's mom. I remember that day very clearly because my husband had written a check for my sister. I handed her the check. It was for one of her paintings. I had begged my husband to buy it for me. My sister gave me a hefty discount as Christmas was coming up in a few months.

I thought that once I told my husband I had told the police, my life as I knew it would be over. So, I needed to see my sister. I needed to have someone hold me. That was two years before I actually filed for divorce.

My sister left. She and her boyfriend came back for dinner. I think my husband knew something was up because unlike other gatherings we had, he kept touching me. When my sister and her boyfriend left, I asked him why he was on Tinder. He said he wasn't... anymore.

He said that he knew I had discovered him so he deleted it. At this time I did not know what he meant was that he migrated to a different dating app. I said that this was it. If he ever pulled anything like that again I would leave. He said that he understood. I told him I had reported him to the police for the time he had kicked me out of the house. He started to complain about that. He said that I really did not have to do that and I should have talked to him first before making such decisions.

The officer came back a couple of times. My husband was not home. The third time that he knocked on our door; it was before seven in the morning, my husband was still asleep. I woke him up and he told me that I had made our lives difficult, and that I just did not know what I was doing.

He kept the officer waiting for almost an hour. I waited with the officer at the door. I was wearing my husband's clothes, and by the looks of the living room it was clear that I had slept on the couch the night before. I told the officer that we were going to marriage counseling. My husband came down after brushing his teeth, showering, and getting dressed for work. He stood at the bottom of the stairs. The officer faced him. I was sitting on the couch. I could not see his face. The officer was in front of him.

When the officer left I asked why he took so long to come down. He said he needed to go to work, and he needed to get ready. He had a bagel while repeating that I did not really need to call the cops.

As he was blaming me for making his life difficult I kept reviewing that day and the days after. I came back home the morning after he kicked me out. He kept talking to me, and I kept quiet. I kept quiet for the next three days. I remember he was late for work on that third day, and he was repeating that he is going to get fired. He said that he was really late. Honestly I think he was lying, and he probably had a date somewhere in some small town or in the same town he was posted that day.

I texted him to ask if he had gotten fired. He was not. But he did use the opportunity to ask me to have dinner with him. We went out for steak. That was his way of saying he knows he made a mistake. He would buy me steak. Filet mignon, medium rare with a side of mashed potatoes and steamed broccoli.

We had sex that night. Again, I am not sure if I wanted to. The guy had just twisted my arm... I did it anyway. I even wore what he asked me to. I even tried to be okay with him shoving that enormous dildo inside of me, but I could not. I tried.... He even took pictures... just like that it was like we are a very happy couple who enjoy each other's company...

That was his fetish, to look at a vagina getting stretched. He kept watching different videos of it, live ones. And while it is okay to have a fetish sometimes, it felt like he was more interested in porn than his wife. He generally preferred masturbating rather than having sex. His explanation was that with sex there is too much expectation. There is too much pressure, and that he knows he is never going to do it the way I want it.

I was willing to explain what I needed, what I wanted, and what I desired. He was not willing to listen. He took all of it as complaining, nagging, and telling him that he is doing everything wrong. He preferred it if I would just lie there. And most of the time I did.

I was constantly mad at myself. I was angry. Sometimes I did not know why. Now that I look back I realize it was because I did not really want to do what was asked of me in almost all the situations, but I did them anyway because I thought I had to. I just needed to gain the love that kept being promised to me. It was just never delivered.

I used to read to him before bed, sometimes lying on my belly, naked. I think I should point out that I can only fall asleep if I am naked. There were many nights when he would just jump on top of my back without asking or any foreplay and just fuck me. I kept reading. I would just freeze. I did not know what else to do. If I would happen to say anything he would make me pay, usually by taking a piece of me away from me. He would take away things I enjoyed. He would suddenly become allergic to something. Etc.

One time after he was done I went to that bathroom and he followed me. He was smiling. He looked at me and he said "you look shocked", more of an observation of that one moment than a realization. He was too involved with himself to actually notice that I had been in a state of shock for months.

I **WAS** shocked. I did not know this man at all. The same man who kept asking me if I was okay more than ten times when we had sex for the first time, was now repeatedly entering me without asking permission. I felt detached rather than connected. I was reliving my past traumas in the relationship I was supposed to feel safe in.

Even the bed I slept in was not safe. Once he had decided it was time for sleep, if I moved, even an inch, he would start yelling and swearing at me. I had to choose a position to lay in and stay like that for the rest of the night. It was a lot of pressure, to the point that I could not fall asleep. What happened was that I spent most of my marriage on a couch either reading or listening to something. I became productive in a lot of ways. My way of coping with all the things happening to me was to work harder, I had to learn more. A part of me thinks that it is all because my parents both believed education is the way to freedom. This has been engraved in my soul. My reaction to most things is to learn more.

His reaction to my books though was to make fun of them. if he did not recognize the title, it must be a stupid book. One book in particular, I remember, he looked at my newly purchased book and said: "you wasted more money on your stupid books again?" and I said: "which *stupid* book are you talking about?" I tried to mimic his tone as I called my own book stupid.

"That one. There is no dance in the title, how do you need that for your research? Do you just buy whatever you think sounds smart" "Do you know who Sir John Malcolm[4] is?" And of course he did not!

It was not just the big stuff, but also little stuff like calling my books stupid was what would make me hesitant when he claimed he loved me. He kept telling me that he loved me after we got married, and I never once felt loved... I felt that I had to prove I care and I love him, but he did not feel any obligation to show his love for me in any way. He said that he was always too sick from my stuff to have any energy to do anything when he came home. He said that I was too much. That I had too many emotions and there was not enough space for his emotions.

I felt guilty feeling my emotions. He would get mad at me if I showed any reaction to his actions. He wanted to feel his feelings and just fly off the handle but he did not want me to have a reflection of any sort to whatever he was doing or saying. I had to listen. I had to take it. I could not tell him how I was feeling or I would have been in trouble. He would turn it around and throw it at my face any chance he would have gotten.

He wanted me to learn the video games he played, so we could "spend time" with each other. I tried to learn, he was a horrible teacher. He kept yelling at me, and when his explanations would not make sense to me he would yell them louder with the same words and order. He kept calling me stupid for not getting such simple things and then he would be even angrier if I wanted to stop playing.

Playing video games was the only thing that he did. He would get up, eat his bagel, go to work, come back, and play video games. Sometimes he even played before going to work. If you are wondering where he got the bagels, I must tell you that I did all the shopping for the house.

I did the shopping. I did the cleaning. I did the laundry. I did the dishes. It is important to add that I of course did them all wrong. But it was not wrong enough for him to want to do them himself. He just took the liberty of reminding me that he knows better than me.

He said that he was allergic to the dishwasher so I had to wash everything by hand. Why did I have to do that you ask. He said that since he was making the money, I had to do the cleaning and everything else around the house.

At some point I got really tired of doing the dishes by hand. So I would put them in the dishwasher, and set them on the counter pretending that I washed them by hand. He never once showed an allergic reaction.

One time he came home before I had a chance to set the dishes on the counter, and he got sick! He said this has happened because I was too lazy to do a simple task. And then he just kept "getting sick". Until one day I started washing the dishes by hand in front of him, and suddenly it was all fine and dandy again.

I have this habit that if the house is not tidy or if there are dishes in the sink I cannot focus on the work that I am doing. He knew this, so he would never do anything. He knew that if he waited long enough I would do it all. He would keep using dishes and leaving them in the sink especially if he had a day off. I think he just wanted to torture me.

One time I had gotten so tired of cleaning that I let go. I did not change the trash bags and they were just overflowing. There was trash on the floor around them. He did not budge. I think on day three maybe he asked if I was done protesting. Then he laughed hysterically and asked me to clean the house.

Towards the end of our marriage I stopped paying attention to things like the sink. And it was easier to do that in the Dallas apartment that we had because the kitchen was separated from the living room with a wall. So, I drank tea and I left my mug in the sink. And he kept drinking tea and leaving his mugs in the sink.

Days went by. At some point he got frustrated that the mugs were all dirty. So, he washed a couple for himself and then he set the rest of them in the trash can. He was trying to teach me a lesson, that was his explanation when I asked why.

He just kept pushing the envelope. When would I get mad enough to leave? Sometimes I think that he was testing me. "How much can I shit all over her before she actually shits back?" I wonder if he asked himself that.

I look back and I ask myself how could I have ever loved anyone like that? Was it love? Was it some twisted version of it that I was taught by being raised in an oppressive environment? I should have known better. But I didn't. I did not know any better. I was isolated, and I did not have anyone.

Most of the time, I would find out about his affairs after they had happened. Now that I look back I think he wanted it that way. It was like reminding me that he is choosing me every time. The last affair he had was different. I think he was still trying to push the envelope further.

One night he came home from work, still afloat. He said: "I think one of the techs really likes me at this store." "Oh, yeah?" was my response. A few days later he mentioned casually that they might need a staff pharmacist in the store he mentioned a few days before. "With the tech?" I asked. He giggled.

"I put in a request to become the pharmacist for the store I talked about." He informed me a few days later. At this point he had been to the store a couple of more times and it seemed that he had flirted with said tech. And he got the job, which of course gave him more reasons to be an asshole. He was doing more work, he was getting paid less. He had to actually take care of the store, but now he was not getting paid for the extra hours or the time he took to get to the store.

I was an easy target. At this point I was scared enough that I did not really complain anymore. I just took it. I did not question him when he said that he is casually going out with the tech. He said it was just coffee and he will be home by ten the latest. He came home at four in the morning.

He came home one day, and he said that he thinks we should have an open marriage because he had never had anyone be interested in him and now that someone is interested in him he wants to give it a shot.

I was amazed, truly. I laughed. I said that I was interested in him. "I married you! I fell for you and I married you! I am still married to you. What do you mean no one has ever been interested in you? Do you think that when I leave this house every day to go anywhere, no one looks at me? Do you realize that loyalty is a choice?"

He giggled. I said: "You do realize that when you say open marriage it means I too get to have relationships with other men, right?" He said that he understood. "Just to be clear, I do not want to have an open marriage. I do not think you should go out with this child or sleep with her. If you do so, I will do so too. Do you understand this?" He said that he fully understood the agreement.

I think what he did not understand about the idea of an open marriage or the idea of polyamory is that as his wife I would be his primary partner. To him though I was someone who cleaned the house as he refused to have sex with me or even touch me because, and I quote: "I am having a committed relationship with my girlfriend."

Now that I look back and analyze the past, I realize every time he was dating someone the frequency of which he touched me became less, and he refused to engage in anything sexual with me. I was always the other woman in my own marriage. I was something, not even someone, he could just fall back on in between his relationships.

He became bold. He would stand me up. Ask me to be ready to go out and never show up. He would come back home at odd hours. He would not pick up his phone if and when I called. He refused to give me his work schedule because he thought it was some sort of a way of controlling him. One time he even told me: " if you come home and there is another woman here, do not tell her you are my wife. Tell her we just live together, we are roommates." He was serious! He actually meant it.

He was dating multiple people he had met on different dating platforms very openly, like it is a thing that everyone does. I am not sure if the kid he was seeing knew this but this was happening at the same time.

And I was an inconvenience in the way of his getting to know all these people...

I remember getting sick. I was vomiting my guts out, and he refused to stay home with me that day. He said the only reason this is happening is because I am a jealous and crazy woman and I have made myself sick so he would not go out with his girlfriend who happens to have an emotional emergency at this moment.

One night he just did not come home. The next morning he shows up to get ready for work. He leaves the house, and a few minutes later he walks back in. He wants to take my car instead of his. Apparently his tire exploded. "Just take my car in and change the tire, I will take your car to work."

I was amazed at the audacity this man possessed. "Why don't you call whoever you were with to come take you to work? She can't just be there for the fun parts." I responded. He started laughing as if I had told a joke. She came to take him to work. He texted me to take the car in and fix it.

I remember this very clearly because it was the Fourth of July weekend. "What is in it for me?" I asked. He got mad that I was taking advantage of him when he needed help. Since he won't be able to take his car in till Tuesday and he needs to go to work on Sunday. The Monday coming up would be the Fourth of July. "I call it negotiating" was my response.

He had gotten used to me just doing whatever he asked over the years of our marriage. I think he did not think it possible that there could be another option, like me having an opinion of my own.

He agreed to have me have his car on the Fourth of July without using my car and let me drive his car when I was visiting my sister at the end of the month in Illinois. He was not happy about it. He made sure he was loud and clear.

I was mad at myself for doing this for him. I do not know why I did. Was I still trying to be the "Good Guy" in the scenario?

Was I hoping serving him in ways he wanted would make him stay in with me instead of taking her on dates and spoiling her?

On Fourth of July I took my own car keys, and I took his car. I went to a friend's house. My husband was furious. When I left he was still asleep. He did not think I would actually take his car when he agreed to let me have his car for Fourth of July. He thought that it was cruel to have taken my own car keys as well. What can I say, my keys are all attached to each other?

On Valentine's Day that year he asked me to wrap the gift he had for her. I was stunned. If you are wondering, I did not do it. At this point I think I had started questioning my loyalties.

"Where is my gift? Where are you taking me?" I asked. Of course no gifts were waiting for me. Why was I still expecting him to suddenly become this thoughtful man when he never was one for me? All the ideas and suggestions I had or brought up were now being done for this teenage girl who had become the center of my husband's attention.

When I asked him why? and how come they are not good ideas for me? he replied: "Well, you taught them to me, I cannot do them for you." He had to use his new tricks on a new female rather than getting better at them with me! I call them tricks because the way he used them degraded them to tricks. They were no longer a way of behavior to me.

What was it that I lacked or did not have that made the man who was married to me pine after another? I wondered almost every day why I was married to him and why he married me in the first place. Yes it would have hurt to break up but it would have been better than this painful marriage. Why did he marry me? Why did he marry me? Why did he marry me?

I never intended on dating anyone while being married still, even though he was sleeping around. It felt wrong. It was two months into his new dating life that he said that I needed to date someone so I would not be so jealous of all the time he is spending with his girlfriend. Also it would help him feel less guilty!

I am saying new dating life because before this girl he would always hide it from me. He did not want me to know. I will never know why he suddenly decided to do this one openly. I wonder though...

He set up a dating profile for me. I think he thought that no one would want me. Or maybe he thought that I did not have it in me to actually do it. I did it. I went out with someone. Well more like going in with someone. The second time I went to see him, I am not sure what took over him, but he suddenly ignored all my requests about using a condom and just fucked me bare.

I went quiet. I froze. I laid there. I actually liked him, you know. I thought if I were to have an affair, this guy could be it. He was handsome enough. Then suddenly he was this man that I was not sure I wanted to be around. I was feeling suffocated. I just wanted to get out of there. I did not want to report him. Because let's face it, it was a weak case. I went there willingly.

I showered at his house after what happened, and I kissed him goodbye.

As the day went by I kept feeling more out of this world. I went home. I cleaned the whole house. I showered again. I then went to pick my husband up from work. As we were watching *Stranger Things* he realized something was wrong with me. He asked what was going on and I showed him the texts I had exchanged with the guy. I had said that I did not know how I felt about him shoving himself inside of me without asking. He had said that it would never happen again.

My husband decided we needed to go to the hospital. We needed to report this. We needed to make sure I did not give him anything. He did not want my discretion to make him get a disease. This coming from a man who had given me multiple infections because he never wore a condom with anybody, made me want to punch him. I did not even have the energy for that though. The thought crossed my mind and I went back to my silence.

He then made me change into a more conservative outfit. He said the way that I dress would make anyone think that I am provoking men at all times. So, I did this to myself because I do not know what to wear when.

We went to the hospital. I cannot even remember the name of the hospital. They said they do not do rape cases here and they sent us to a different hospital. We waited hours before checking in. It was a crucial process. I told them I did not want to report it. And they said that it was okay, but no my husband wanted to report it. He said that I had to.

So I told the nurse that I changed my mind. Why did I do everything that he told me? I sat there for people to come and prey on me. There was no end to the number of the people that kept coming. By the time we were done at the hospital it was about seven in the morning. I was all drugged up. So, when we got home I went to bed.

When I woke up with the need to go to the bathroom, I could not get up. I called for my husband. He was not home. I called again, thinking maybe I wasn't yelling loud enough. Nope. He was not there. I tried to get up. I fell. I tried to get up again. I kept falling. I remember wailing. I was in so much pain, and not just emotionally. To be truly alone is the heaviest pain of all.

He came home maybe around ten at night? I do not recall. What I remember perfectly is the day after. I am lying there on the bed, and he comes and lies next to me. He says: "now that you have been tainted, I think it is better if I move in with my girlfriend."

I think I had a tiny stroke right then and there. My chest hurt so much that I wanted to rip my heart out. I was screaming very loudly but no one could hear. In that moment more than any time in my life all I wanted was my mother. And she was half a world away from me. What I would have given in that moment to have her hold me.

What makes me even sadder is that when the detective decided that I had changed my words and I just did not know what rape is, the people who were there for emotional support stopped responding to my emails.

I had literally no one.

There I was. In a new state, first year PhD student, raped, and left.

He said if I did not sue him he would pay off my car and pay my rent till I graduated. Of course he was lying.... What did I expect?

I said I was going to file for divorce then. He said that I did not have to do that. We will just be separated. He will come back at some point! He said you come live with us!!!! So I do not have to pay two rents. When I refused he changed his words. He said that he said those things under duress. That I had threatened him, and he is only going to pay off the car and only because his name is on the loan. He said that he has always been a good husband and I shouldn't have made a big deal out of this one relationship he wanted to have. He said that everybody cheats and I should just get over it...

All of this was very confusing. One moment he was talking as if we were getting a divorce, the next he was talking as if I would not dare leave because, and I quote: "what are you going to do for food?" he was trying to get me to stay so he would not take a financial blow. So I gave in. I said all I wanted was to get rid of him. And he agreed to sign the divorce decree.

I filed for divorce in August of 2022, and while the clerk was typing I could not stop crying. I stopped when the paperwork was done. Then I met my rebound in the first week of September. I remember things very clearly because my husband hadn't fully moved out yet.

He moved out on September 10th, almost a year after we had moved to Dallas. As he was loading his U-Haul, I told him that I was still willing to forgive but if he moves, this is it, he cannot move back. He said that he understands.

One week later he showed up at my door with lunch. He said he wants to be my husband again because she doesn't know how to love him. He did not say that he misses me. He did not say that he regrets anything. He did not apologize. He said, and I quote: "she doesn't know how to love me." He was the important one. Not the relationship. Not other people involved. HIM.

There was a bouquet of Lilies on the counter. He looked at them and said: "we can have flowers; we can have them on the balcony." So, he was expecting me to move into the apartment he had rented with his GF. All I said was: "I cannot give him up."

My rebound. He was a slightly better version of my husband who drove a Tesla around the DFW area and had a Camry for his road trips, owned two houses in DFW, and constantly complained about being broke. So, now I can see that I should have seen the resemblance there. Both men kept complaining about being broke to a graduate student who literally works in exchange for education.

He was constantly talking about himself and what he was feeling. He had this bracelet that said: "consent is sexy" but he would fuck me even when I had an infection and I was literally telling him to his face that I can't have sex. He would say: "our connection is so strong I cannot stop myself, are you feeling this?" while I was crying under him... nut of course the tears were an orgasm through my eyes!

He would change what he had said a few minutes before, and then yell at me that I am lying to his face about his feelings and actions. One time he decided he needed to do a cleanse by not having sex. Instead of saying that to me he said: "so I am not coming to see you for the next 40 days because I do not want to have sex."

I was his sex toy.

He did not make it to 40 days! When he showed up at my door asking for sex I asked what happened to the cleanse? He said that it was a decision on his part to make it shorter. I can now see the similarities of course. At the time though I was happy enough I had someone who wasn't constantly telling me I was stupid. It felt like a step up when in fact it wasn't.

It was not a super long relationship, that is if we can call it that. Because we only just fucked really, when he wanted....he decided he had a super strong connection with someone else at some point, and when I told him I preferred it if he did

not sleep with this particular person , and of course he did,
He said that he was poly and maybe I was not built for a poly
relationship. I did not have the energy to remind him that even
in a poly relationship there are boundaries defined, that there
are agreements. For example when you agree not to sleep with
someone you need to respect that boundary.

Instead I decided I am done. Though my brain was confused,
I kept texting him even though I knew I did not want to be with
him. And of course he ended up turning it around and kind of
flipping me off.

That is when it hit me.

The emotional burden I had been suppressing for the past
four months.

That what I felt toward this new person was not about him.
It was me still trying to save a relationship with my husband,
the person who treated me so horribly. I did not love this new
person. I was denying my falling out of love with my husband.

I could not stop crying. I was crying day out and night in.
When I was not crying I was sleeping. I was so depressed. I
needed help and I did not have it. Or at least I did not know
where and how to get it.

When I had to call my husband to ask him to meet up and
sign the divorce decree it was one of the hardest things I had
to do. When I entered the pizza shop with him, I felt a shift in
the air around me. I suddenly felt tired. Even being near him
was draining me. He told me he would change, that he would

never cheat on me again, that he would get me an SUV like I had asked.

I just could not be in the same space as him anymore. As hard as it was to think of what a penny life I was being sent off to, I could not bring myself to get back to the stressful life of being his wife. He let me order the biggest pizza, and some sides. He said that he was worried about me and that I never knew how and when to eat.

Then he started crying…

Then I had to beg him to just sign the damn papers.

I cried all the way home. And the day after. And the day after.

I was granted divorce on December 30th 2022.

I started making myself so busy that I could not feel anything anymore. I was scared that any minute he might change his mind. And in the state of Texas you can change your mind up to 30 days after you sign a divorce decree. I counted the days. I really did not want to be attached to him.

I felt lonely. I did. I cried a lot. When I was not crying I was sleeping. And then one day I stopped.

I was happier. I even had a classmate tell me that this semester I look lighter! Like I can walk better!

I look back still and ask myself why I married him when I saw the red flags, why did I think I was any different? I ask myself why it took me so long. I get mad at myself and then I calm myself down.

Because I know now that I deserve better, and yes I stayed, and it took me longer than it should have to leave but I did. I did it. I left! I am out. I gained a life experience that I would not have any other way. I look at love differently now. I understand that love and pain are not necessarily synonyms.

I do not regret my marriage, and I do not regret my divorce. They were the right choices for me at the time.

All I hope is that my pain and suffering helps others to avoid similar situations. All I want is for my pain to have been for a reason...

Notes

[1]Namadi cloth, also known as "namad" or "felt," is a traditional textile in Iran, with a rich history that dates back centuries. It is made through a process of matting, condensing, and pressing fibers together, typically wool, to create a dense, durable fabric. Namadi cloth is not woven but is instead created by manipulating the fibers into a cohesive material using heat, moisture, and pressure

[2]Geleem, also known as Kilims in English, is a traditional flat-woven rug that originates from Iran and other parts of the Middle East. Geleem rugs are distinct from pile carpets, as they are woven without the use of knots, resulting in a thinner, lighter, and more flexible fabric. These

rugs have been an integral part of Persian culture for centuries, known for their vibrant colors, intricate patterns, and cultural significance.

[3]The Guidance Patrol (Persian: ,□□□□□ □□□romanized: gašt-e eršâd) or morality police is an Islamic religious police force and vice squad in the Law Enforcement Command of the Islamic Republic of Iran.morality police, law enforcement body in Iran created in 2005 to enforce regulations on modest dress (ḥijāb) and chaste behavior ('ifāf). The enforcement of a public moral code in Iran began after the 1979 revolution, when the new Islamic republic sought to assert its ideology and principles in public spaces.

[4]Major-General Sir John Malcolm GCB, KLS (2 May 1769 – 30 May 1833) was a Scottish soldier, diplomat, East India Company administrator, statesman, and historian. The book he was pointing to was Sketches of Persia (1827) – this book is not written by Malcolm, but by one of his companions in his mission to Iran; the writer

remains anonymous and has introduced himself as the traveler; he has referred to Malcolm in his text as ilch, which is a Persian word meaning envoy of a foreign country

Acknowledgments

First and foremost, I want to express my heartfelt gratitude to my beta readers for dedicating their time and energy to read and provide feedback on my work. Thank you, Joel Heimerman, for your patience in reading and rereading and rereading the manuscript. Cynthia Miller, I truly appreciate your meticulous checking of every detail. Rachel Lara, your thoughtful and respectful critique is invaluable; I admire your skill in providing feedback with sensitivity. Evan Roberts, I'm grateful for your candidness and willingness to voice confusion when needed.

Thank you also to the gracious instructor and classmates of Creativity as Social Practice for the feedback you gave on my performance of this manuscript when it was in its infancy, and only four pages long, as a one-woman show. Your questions and insight helped me improve and expand the manuscript to a six-page monologue.

This expanded monologue was performed at the Coalescence Theatre Project in the Augusto Boal style, which encouraged the audience to interrupt the performance. Thank you to all those who helped me produce this performance. And thanks to the wonderful audience that was there—some of you knew my ex-husband and me. Your feedback and clarifying questions helped me further improve the script.

A wholehearted thank you to Kee-Yoon Nahm. Thank you for reading the monologue when it was a short version and asking me the right questions which guided me to what is now a longer version.

I also want to extend my deepest thanks to my wonderful sister, Shahrbanoo Hamzeh, for the brilliant painting that graces the cover. It perfectly captures the essence of the story I am telling. I'm incredibly proud to have you as both my sister and a talented artist in my life.

I want to thank the amazing Rose for taking the time to design the cover and help bring this project to fruition.

Last but not least (in some ways), I want to thank my ex-husband for giving me the experience to be able to write this manuscript. Not that I am happy to have been through hell; I am grateful that it has helped me grow.

I am truly fortunate to have such remarkable people in my life.

I count my blessings every day.

About The Author

Shahrzad Hamzeh lives in Dallas, Texas where she is studying for her PhD in visual and performing arts. She was born and raised in Iran where she first discovered her love of dance but soon learned she would not be allowed to pursue her passions while living under the regime of the Islamic Republic. Coming to America opened up new opportunities, but forced her to leave behind family and friends, as well as a culture and a people that she loves and cares for deeply.

Her writing is a way to create connections between her experiences as a Persian woman, immigrant, survivor, student, daughter, sister and dancer. Alongside her PhD work she is currently writing a full-length memoir of her life in Iran. The Rant is her first published book.